AMERICAN HERITAGE
ILLUSTRATED HISTORY
OF THE UNITED STATES

U.S. Secretary of State Henry Kissinger meets with Chairman Mao Tse-tung in Beijing in February 1973.
XINHUA NEWS AGENCY

FRONT COVER: *American G.I.'s disembark from a helicopter in the Vietnamese jungle in the early 1970s.*
DEPARTMENT OF DEFENSE

FRONT ENDSHEET: *A Strategic Air Command B-52 bombs a Vietcong stronghold.*
OFFICIAL U.S. AIR FORCE PHOTO

CONTENTS PAGE: *Earth Day, April 22, 1970, turned the nation's attention to the issue of the environment. Here, demonstrators take over New York's Fifth Avenue.*
PHOTO TRENDS

BACK ENDSHEET: *President Richard Nixon visits the Great Wall during his 1972 trip to China.*
NATIONAL ARCHIVES

BACK COVER: *Astronaut Edwin E. Aldrin Jr. (top) stands beside the U.S. flag that was planted on the moon in 1969; Rev. Martin Luther King, Jr., arrives at the Alabama State Capitol (bottom left) after his historic civil-rights march in 1965; the first nationwide peace demonstration (bottom right), in October, 1969, was mounted in response to escalation of the war in Vietnam.*
NASA; PHOTO TRENDS; UPI

AMERICAN HERITAGE ILLUSTRATED HISTORY OF THE UNITED STATES

VOLUME 17

THE VIETNAM ERA

BY MEDIA PROJECTS INCORPORATED

Created in Association with the
Editors of AMERICAN HERITAGE

CHOICE PUBLISHING, INC.
New York

Library of Congress Catalog Card Number: 87-73399
ISBN 0-945260-17-2

This 1988 edition is published and distributed by Choice Publishing, Inc., 53 Watermill Lane, Great Neck, NY 11021
by arrangement with American Heritage, a division of Forbes, Inc.

Manufactured in the United States of America

CONTENTS OF THE COMPLETE SERIES

Editor's Note to the Revised Edition
Introduction by ALLAN NEVINS
Main text by MEDIA PROJECTS INCORPORATED

EACH VOLUME CONTAINS AN ENCYCLOPEDIC SECTION; MASTER INDEX IN VOLUME 18

CONTENTS OF VOLUME 17

CHAPTER 49

ESCALATION AND QUAGMIRE

Few Americans knew much about Vietnam when it first began appearing in the headlines in the 1960s. Long dominated by an oppressive French colonial government, Vietnam had been overrun by the Japanese in their conquest of Southeast Asia during the early days of World War II. French control was reestablished after the Japanese defeat, but the French were not long able to contend with a growing Vietnamese rebellion against foreign domination. The Vietnamese, led by Ho Chi Minh and supported by the Soviet Union and Communist China, stepped up their attacks on the French until in May, 1954, they achieved a stunning victory, overwhelming a French force of 15,000 troops at the town of Dien Bien Phu. At subsequent peace talks in Geneva, Vietnam was divided at the 17th parallel. North of that line Ho Chi Minh's Communist government retained power; in South

American G.I.'s disembark from a helicopter in the Vietnamese jungle in the early 1970s.

Vietnam, a nationalist government was established under French control.

The Geneva accords provided for the transfer of power from the French to an elected Vietnamese government that would unify both north and south. But this was not to happen. While Ho Chi Minh consolidated his power in the north, the South Vietnamese government under Ngo Dinh Diem began to falter. Rigged elections kept him in power, but reforms he had promised were never carried out, and Communist Viet Cong Guerrillas, supported by North Vietnam, became increasingly active. The last French troops were withdrawn from Vietnam in early 1956.

"I can conceive of no greater tragedy than for the United States to become involved in an all-out war in Asia," President Eisenhower had declared. Nevertheless, his administration provided substantial financial aid to the South Vietnamese, and at Diem's request, the number of U.S. military advisers was increased from 327 to 685 in

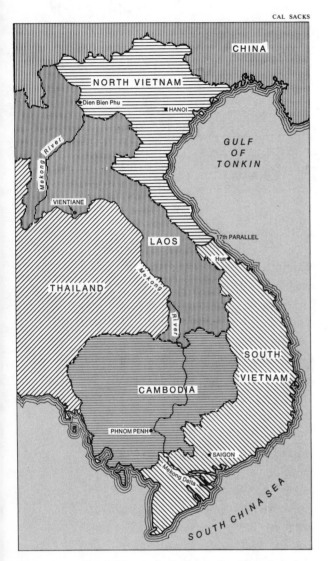

South Vietnam's fate was considered vital to all Indochina when war erupted.

May, 1960. It was a relatively small number, but with an increasingly unstable government in South Vietnam, a Communist menace in the north, and the beginnings of a U.S. military presence, the stage was set for an American commitment that would ultimately prove disastrous.

This commitment deepened during the Kennedy administration, fueled by the young President's belief that Americans must be willing to "pay any price, bear any burden...oppose any foe" to "assure the survival and...success of liberty." By 1963, the year of Kennedy's assassination, there were more than 16,000 military advisers serving in Vietnam. And they were making command decisions in the field, flying air-support missions, and providing fire support and reconnaissance at sea. As early as 1962, it was clear to James Reston of *The New York Times* that "the United States is now involved in an undeclared war in South Vietnam."

This undeclared war expanded still more rapidly under Lyndon Johnson. In August, 1964, torpedo boats from North Vietnam attacked two American destroyers in the Gulf of Tonkin.

The Tonkin Resolution

Within a week of the incident, Johnson had secured from Congress a joint resolution authorizing him to "take all necessary measures" to repel armed attacks against American forces in Vietnam and, more important, "to prevent further aggression." This amounted practically to a military carte blanche. The authorization was used gingerly at first. Gradually, however, it was interpreted to cover not only retaliatory raids upon northern military installations but also strategic bombing of the North Vietnamese industrial war machine and transportation network. By February, 1965, air sorties against North Vietnam had become routine. Four months later, after the appearance of North Vietnamese regulars on South Vietnamese soil, American troops now numbering some 50,000 men were shifted from advisory to combat status.

As Vietnam became more and more an American enterprise, the United States pressed repeatedly on the diplomatic front for negotiations that might end the conflict. On the war front, the Johnson administration engaged in a kind of carrot-and-stick strategy. Repeatedly, the President ordered temporary halts to the bombing raids on the North, while peace feelers were put out. With each rebuff, the war effort escalated. Two years after the Tonkin Gulf incident, U.S. forces were in excess of 350,000, and war deaths had risen to more than 6,500. As the war expanded, it also became more difficult to understand. There were few clear-cut battles or victories in the traditional military sense. The enemy seemed to be everywhere, setting out booby traps and land mines, lying in ambush, attacking in brief, fierce firefights, then melting back into the lush, deceptively beautiful countryside. American and South Vietnamese soldiers retaliated with "search and destroy" missions, and were dropped in and taken back out of battle aboard chattering helicopters. For the non-Communist forces, body counts, rather than ground gained, became the measure of success.

Massacre at My Lai

To the Americans, the Viet Cong were often indistinguishable from the South Vietnamese farmers among whom they hid, and in the efforts to flush them out, innocent villages were sometimes burned and women and children killed. In the most shocking American atrocity of the war, a platoon led by Army Lieutenant William L. Calley, Jr., stormed into the village of My Lai on March 16, 1968, and shot indiscriminately at men, women, and children as

Saigon, the beautiful capital of South Vietnam, became the scene of intense fighting between Vietcong guerrillas and U.S. and South Vietnamese troops during the Tet Offensive of 1968.

A North Vietnamese torpedo boat attacks an American destroyer in the South China Sea in August, 1964. This incident led to the passage of the Gulf of Tonkin Resolution, which gave President Lyndon Johnson the authority to wage war in Southeast Asia.

United States Marines search for Vietcong in a marsh in South Vietnam. Nearly 550,000 American servicemen were stationed in that divided country by the spring of 1968.

they ran from their huts. Some survivors were captured, led to a ditch, and executed. Almost nine months passed before news of the My Lai massacre reached the outside world. Although the exact number of people executed by Calley and his men was never accurately determined, he was charged with responsibility for 102 deaths when he was finally brought to trial, and was convicted of killing 22.

By 1967, the Vietnamese war had become the single most important issue in the United States, and its drain upon the country's human and economic resources had eroded the consensus President Johnson had tried to maintain since taking office. The first of his domestic policies to lose support was his system of wage-price guidelines. Under them, there had been tacit but substantial agreement among government, labor, and management that prices of basic commodities would be held relatively stable and that wage increases would be kept close to the estimated annual rise of worker productivity—roughly 3%. Basic steel prices led the breakdown when they rose to $14 a ton. A series of wage increases ranging up to 8% soon followed, and inflation, creeping along at a relatively stable 2% annually, broke into a gallop. The consumer price index indicated a 4% price rise in 1967, and by that summer, Johnson was forced to ask Congress for a 10% income-tax surcharge to dampen the inflationary surge and to cover the mounting costs of the Vietnam conflict. Meanwhile, antiwar sentiment in Congress grew stronger.

Senator J. William Fulbright (Democrat, Arkansas), chairman of the Senate Foreign Relations Committee, questioned Johnson's broad interpretation of the Tonkin Gulf Resolution. Senator Robert F. Kennedy (Democrat, New York), the late President's brother, called for an end to the bombing of North Vietnam. In the nation's colleges and universities, a new generation of young people was becoming politically active. Many had taken part in civil–rights marches and demonstrations in 1963 and 1964. Now they turned their attention to ending the war.

Antiwar protests

The first rumblings of discontent had emerged at the University of California at Berkeley in the fall of 1964. The issue in the beginning was the right of students to advocate their concerns outside the main gate of the university, but the "Free Speech" movement expanded rapidly, drawing in a number of faculty members as well as students and focusing on issues beyond the university community. As one observer noted, "A rebellion was already in being and searching for a cause." The radicals from Berkeley carried out their first antiwar demonstrations at the Oakland army terminal in October, 1965. On October 23, the son of a Berkeley faculty member burned his draft card, the first reported instance of a type of protest that was soon to sweep the country. Students at the University of Michigan developed the "teach-in" in March, 1965, as a method of focusing "attention on the

President Lyndon Johnson and Soviet Premier Aleksei Kosygin in Glassboro, New Jersey, in June, 1967. Their meeting was helpful, but produced no concrete results.

war, its consequences, and ways to stop it.'' By November, 1965, the student movement had gathered enough strength to lead an antiwar protest in Washington that drew between 15,000 and 25,000 people.

Meanwhile, sentiment began to arise in the black community that the war was siphoning off resources vital to the anti-poverty effort. Despite great advances in civil rights, black Americans still faced substantial discrimination in housing, jobs, and pay. In August, 1965, rioting in Watts, an impoverished, predomi-nantly black section of Los Angeles, left

35 dead and hundreds injured. It was the first of several urban uprisings over the next two years that were rooted in black frustration over the deepening poverty of lives spent trapped in decaying city ghet-tos.

Still seeking another avenue of peace in the Vietnam conflict, President John-son met with Premier Aleksei Kosygin of the Soviet Union at Glassboro State College in New Jersey in June, 1967. The Soviet Union was supplying the North Vietnamese, and it was hoped that the Soviet government could use its influence to bring Hanoi to the confer-

Anti-American demonstrations have occurred often in both friendly and unfriendly countries. Here, the Chinese Red Guards attack U.S. "imperialism."

EASTFOTO

ence table. The U.S.S.R., however, was engaged in an ideological war with Communist China, and any overt efforts on the Soviet's part to help with the peace effort would be immediately poisoned by Chinese propaganda.

In addition, the worldwide competition between the two superpowers had found another explosive outlet in the Middle East. There, Arab power, centered in President Gamal Abdel Nasser's Egypt, confronted the small but highly developed state of Israel. Since his rise to power in the early 1950s, Nasser had sought to rally the Arab world behind him by making both a religious and territorial issue of Israel. An uneasy truce, supervised by the United Nations, had prevailed for more than a decade, but now Nasser, lavishly equipped by the Soviets, felt ready to move. In May, 1967, gathering Syria and Jordan to his cause, Nasser occupied the disputed Gaza Strip on the Mediterranean coast, closed the Gulf of Aqaba east of Suez to Israeli shipping, and ordered the U.N. truce force to leave the area. Israel, in a lightning display of military power, destroyed the Egyptian air force, retook the Gaza Strip, occupied the Jordanian half of Jerusalem as well as the strategic Golan Heights, in southwestern Syria, and drove through the Sinai Penninsula

to the Suez Canal. The United States and the Soviet Union took steps to reassure each other they would not intervene while their surrogates battled. However, the war was over in six days, and to the acute embarrassment of the Soviet Union, the Egyptian fighting potential lay strewn in ruins around Israel's widened borders.

The Tet Offensive

As America entered the election year of 1968, the Vietnam War was costing around $25,000,000,000 a year. Inflationary pressures were increasing. War deaths had risen past 15,000, and troop commitments stood at more than 475,000—more men than America had sent to Korea at the height of that conflict. Military assurances that the United

1451

South Vietnam's National Police Chief, Nguyen Ngoc Loan, executes a Viet Cong officer in Saigon during the Tet Offensive of 1968. Run on the front page of many American newspapers and on network television, this photograph dramatically galvanized public opinion against the war.

States was winning were seriously undermined on January 30, when the Communists launched an offensive against the major cities of South Vietnam during Tet, the Vietnamese lunar New Year. Thirty-six provincial capitals were hit; so were 72 district towns, plus airfields, combat bases, and military headquarters. Fourteen thousand people were killed, 22,000 were wounded, and half a million new refugees were driven from their homes. But from the point of view of the American public, the most unsettling attack was made at Saigon, by a 17-man Vietcong squad that managed to get inside the American embassy compound before they were shot down. The Tet offensive was eventually beaten back, but television images of the street fighting persuaded many Americans that the war was not going as well as the government had claimed. The Johnson administration's reaction was both to raise troop commitments to nearly 550,000 and to press efforts to hold peace talks.

The seizure by North Koreans of the American intelligence ship U.S.S. *Pueblo* in the Sea of Japan on January 23, 1968, further exposed the apparent powerlessness of the United States to deal decisively with small belligerent powers in the Nuclear Age.

On March 31, President Johnson announced the unilateral cessation of bombing missions over 90% of North Vietnam. He called upon Hanoi to respond to this new initiative. Then, dramatically, he relieved the gesture of any suggestion that it was prompted by election-year political motives: ''I shall not seek, and I will not accept the nomination of my party for another term as your President.'' Johnson, in short, had sacrificed his remarkable political career in an all-out gamble to bring Hanoi to the conference table. At last the Communists responded, and negotiations between North Vietnam and the United States were arranged. Talks opened in Paris on May 10, but the heavy toll of the war hardly abated. The Tet offensive and a follow-up series of attacks in May had proved costly to the Communists. Nevertheless, the attacks had also brought American battle deaths since 1961 to more than 25,000.

The crises at home

The war continued to work its evils at home, contributing to a mounting debate over the nation's moral values, and angry domestic divisions increased. Black communities in cities across the nation had revolted violently during the ''long, hot summer'' of 1967. The worst race riot in the nation's history had gripped Detroit, where 43 people died and $200,000,000 in damage was done in

In the mid-1960s, Black frustrations turned into violence. Scores of cities, such as Detroit above in July 1967, turned into riot-torn battlefields.

five days of violence. In early 1968, the President's Commission on Civil Disorder reported pointedly that the nation showed disturbing signs of splitting into "two Americas, one black and one white," and recommended that the highest possible priority be given to closing the gap between the lofty expectations of the poor and the grim reality of their lives.

Meanwhile, militancy among college students—most calling for civil rights and demanding an end to the war, some also revolting against the whole value system they saw as the Establishment—further widened what had come to be called the Generation Gap.

Even in the normally calm center of the American political spectrum, corrosive forces were at work. Inflation, the human sacrifices of the war, student alienation, and the economic and emotional anxieties of life in the decaying cities all combined to raise questions about the quality of American leadership and the effectiveness of the nation's institutions.

Picking a president

Thus beset, Americans turned to the task of selecting candidates for the 1968 Presidential election. Lyndon Johnson's decision to withdraw from the race had been prompted in part by the emergence of two strong antiwar contenders in his own party. Senator Eugene J. McCarthy (Democrat, Minnesota) had astonished him and other party leaders by winning 42% of the Democratic vote in the bellwether New Hampshire primary. McCarthy's erudite assault on the war on both moral and practical grounds had attracted to his cause an eager corps of young college-educated adherents. Perhaps more important, it had helped persuade another, potentially still more powerful rival for the Presidency, Robert F. Kennedy, to run for the office his brother had so recently held. LBJ's unexpected retreat from the field initiated a wide-open primary struggle among McCarthy, Kennedy, and Johnson's Vice-President, former Senator Hubert H. Humphrey of Minnesota, once a voluble leader of the party's liberal wing but now a supporter of his President's policies in Southeast Asia.

To further complicate the political picture, the Democratic Governor of Alabama, George C. Wallace, announced his independent candidacy, with retired Air Force General Curtis LeMay as his running mate. Wallace hoped to appeal beyond the borders of Dixie, where he had first become known as a strident, last-ditch segregationist, to disaffected northerners made uneasy by racial strife and urban street crime. Even the simple phrase "law and order" took on an anti-black connotation, and Americans about to choose their new leader found they could no longer count on a common language. Slogans and code words now meant different things, not only from region to region, but from neighborhood to neighborhood. The rents in the American fabric widened further in April when Dr. Martin Luther King, Jr., charismatic and highly effective leader of the non-violent civil–rights movement, was murdered by a white sniper in Memphis, Tennessee, setting off a new firestorm of

Many of the refugees fleeing Saigon were members of South Vietnam's military establishment. Here, a South Vietnamese helicopter pilot, with his wife and child, is escorted to safety aboard a U.S. aircraft carrier during the evacuation of Saigon, in April, 1975.

The Reverend Martin Luther King, Jr., and President Lyndon Johnson confer in the White House prior to the signing of the Voting Rights Act of 1965.

violence in and around the country's ghettos. Thirty-seven people died as rioting erupted again in a hundred cities and towns.

Then, after winning the California primary, in June, Robert Kennedy was assassinated in the kitchen of a Los Angeles hotel by a troubled Palestinian immigrant. For the first time since the Civil War, it seemed to some in the turbulent spring and summer of 1968 that the American center could not hold.

Chicago convention riots

The Democratic convention in August was a disaster for the party, not so much because of what happened inside the Chicago Amphitheatre as because of the appalling violence in the streets outside. On the evening of August 29, as the delegates prepared to pick their nominee, thousands of antiwar demonstrators massed along Michigan Avenue in front of Humphrey headquarters in the Hilton Hotel in full view of television cameras.

Suddenly, the police began to beat back the crowd, using nightsticks, mace,

Cut down by an assassin's bullet in Memphis, Tennessee, the Reverend Martin Luther King, Jr. was buried in Atlanta, Georgia, on April 9, 1968. Here, his casket is borne to the grave on a wooden farm wagon.

1457

and tear gas; a nonpartisan panel later declared the event had been "a police riot." Hundreds of protestors were hurt, some seriously, as they chanted, "the whole world is watching."

The live pictures of bleeding young people relayed into millions of American homes that night ensured that the election of 1968 would in part be a referendum on the conduct of the Vietnam War and how best to deal with the domestic violence it had helped to spawn. In Miami, the Republicans quietly picked former Vice-President Richard M. Nixon and Maryland Governor Spiro T. Agnew as their candidates.

The nomination of Hubert Humphrey for President and Senator Edmund Muskie of Maine for Vice-President struck many Democrats as a bitter anti-climax. And the stalled peace talks at Paris, which since May had failed to bring any measurable reduction in the fighting in Vietnam, seemed to ensure that the Democratic nominees would be forced to campaign in favor of policies that fewer and fewer members of their own party found to their liking.

The 1968 campaign

In the campaign, both Nixon and Humphrey—equally experienced and astute in the arts of elective politics—sought to rally the crumbling, elusive center of the American political system. Each approached the task from a different direction.

Humphrey, burdened with the Johnson administration's war policy and the riotous debacle of the Chicago convention, pinned his strategic hopes on a coalition of big-city election machinery, the black vote, the progressive traditions of labor, and the moderate sentiments of the middle class. The traditionally Democratic Southern conservative vote was lost, in his view, to the third-party candidate, George C. Wallace.

Nixon, on the other hand, sought to draw the moderately conservative border states, the farm vote, and the suburbs of the major cities into a new coalition. He viewed this coalition as committed to an orderly settlement of the Vietnam issue and a less turbulent approach to civil–rights matters. He was successful, but not overwhelmingly so. The popular vote was surprisingly close, with the Republican Nixon-Agnew ticket winning 31,785,480 votes and the Democratic Humphrey-Muskie slate winning 31,275,166, a difference of only 510,314 out of more than 70 million ballots cast. The Nixon-Agnew team lost every major city in the nation, but captured such key states as California, Illinois, and Indiana to win an electoral majority of 301 votes in 32 states. Humphrey and Muskie received 191 votes in 13 states and the District of Columbia. The Wallace strategy failed to carry a single Northern or border state. He did, however, capture Alabama, Arkansas, Georgia, Louisiana, and Mississippi, with their 46 electoral votes. Moreover, his 9,906,473 popular votes were the most in history for a third-party candidate.

But the Vietnam War still raged on, and the deep emotional and intellectual divisions among American citizens were yet to be healed.

VIETNAM:
THE WAR IN COLOR

The Vietnam War was covered more extensively by the media than any previous American conflict. With virtually no military censorship of the press, reporters and television crews roamed the country at will. Advances in technology allowed instant communication with the United States. Moreover, military journalists and photographers documented every aspect of the American presence in Vietnam for Department of Defense records. Television brought the war home, broadcast live in family rooms around the nation.

Many historians and critics have credited the media with hastening the end of American involvement in Vietnam. Certainly the shocking and brutal images relayed back from the battlefields and the war-torn cities and villages helped erode whatever enthusiasm Americans had for the conflict. Perhaps the high point of the media's influence came in the wake of the Tet Offensive, when the trusted television anchorman Walter Cronkite announced that the war was at a "stalemate." This admission, flying in the face of the optimistic reports of American commanders, is credited with triggering a major shift in American public opinion. The pictures in this section, both the famous and the lesser known, are a small part of the mosaic of images that represent the Vietnam War.

OFFICIAL U.S. ARMY PHOTO

At first considered useless in the Vietnamese jungle, tanks and armored vehicles emerged as a major force in American operations. Here, an M-551 Assault Vehicle and its crew await instructions on a reconnaissance mission.

AMERICA STEPS IN

An American adviser and his Vietnamese counterpart inspect an ARVN (Army of the Republic of Vietnam) unit on the outskirts of Saigon. After the French left Vietnam in the mid-1950s, the United States took on the responsibility of arming and advising the military forces of South Vietnam.

Years before American troops arrived in large numbers—which began in 1965—U.S. Army Special Forces (popularly known as Green Berets after their distinctive headgear) were operating in Vietnam. Often working with primitive Montagnard tribes in Vietnam's highlands, they established camps like the one above to protect civilians from Vietcong harassment and provide a base for counter-guerrilla operations. The photo shows the camp's defensive perimeter, with machine-gun and mortar emplacements. To the north is the camp's airstrip.

With its wide boulevards and graceful buildings, Saigon, South Vietnam's capital and largest city, was sometimes called the Paris of the Orient. It is shown here in a relatively peaceful period. Saigon was renamed Ho Chi Minh City, in honor of the North Vietnamese leader, after it fell to the Communists in 1975.

Hue, the seat of Vietnam's ancient emperors, was considered the most beautiful city in the nation. A symbol of the Vietnamese people's history and culture, it was reduced to ruins in the 1968 Tet Offensive, when U.S. and ARVN troops fought a brutal 25-day battle to drive Communist forces from the city.

Buddhist monks, such as those shown here, were outspoken in their opposition to the corrupt Diem regime which ruled South Vietnam in the late 1950s and early 1960s. Several burned themselves to death in protest against the Catholic Ngo Dinh Diem's repression of South Vietnam's mostly Buddhist population.

AMERICAN TROOPS ON THE GROUND

OFFICIAL U.S. ARMY PHOTO

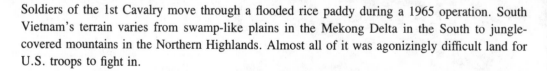

Soldiers of the 1st Cavalry move through a flooded rice paddy during a 1965 operation. South Vietnam's terrain varies from swamp-like plains in the Mekong Delta in the South to jungle-covered mountains in the Northern Highlands. Almost all of it was agonizingly difficult land for U.S. troops to fight in.

The Iron Triangle, a heavily forested area near Saigon, was infested with Vietcong tunnels. Left, a specially trained "tunnel rat" of the 25th Division emerges from the earth during "Operation Atlanta," in 1967. The Vietcong made extensive use of underground passages to hide from American and ARVN troops.

A GI of the 4th Division guards Vietcong captured in a 1970 operation. The elusive Vietcong guerrillas preferred ambushes and booby traps to conventional battles. Operating from tunnels or the jungle and easily blending in with civilians, they were difficult to capture.

It was the ordinary Marine or Army infantryman—the "grunt"—who bore the heaviest burden of combat in Vietnam. Below, a paratrooper shouts for a medic during the fierce battle of Dak To, in 1967.

WAR BY HELICOPTER

The helicopter is perhaps the most persistent image of the Vietnam War. Vast numbers of them were available for American forces, and the versatile aircraft were used to do everything from transporting men and supplies to attacking enemy positions.

Wounded soldiers from the battle of Dak To, left, are evacuated from a devastated jungle clearing. Unarmed Med-Evac helicopters operated as flying ambulances, often braving fierce enemy fire to quickly bring wounded troops from the bush to hospitals in the rear. Wounded men thus stood a better chance of survival than in previous wars.

OFFICIAL U.S. ARMY PHOTO

OFFICIAL U.S. ARMY PHOTO

With their speed, maneuverability, and capacity to land troops virtually anywhere, helicopters gave American forces a high degree of mobility. Whole units, such as the Army's "airmobile" 1st Cavalry, could be brought into or withdrawn from remote battle zones in a matter of hours. Right, engineers of the 1st Division descend a rope ladder to clear a landing zone for the helicopters carrying the division's assault troops.

Left, a UH-18 gunship strafes a Vietcong position in the highlands. Helicopters armed with rockets, machine guns, and cannons were used to provide close support for ground troops. Helicopters were also used by observers to spot targets for artillery fire, and American commanders directed operations from Command-and-Control helicopters high above the battlefield.

VIETNAM: THE WAR IN COLOR

FIRE FROM THE SKIES

A suspected Vietcong base just north of Saigon burns after being hit by white phosphorous chemical bombs by Air Force B-52 bombers. The enormous B-52's, usually based in the Philippines or Thailand, flew so high that they could not be heard on the ground.

Napalm, a highly flammable compound of jellied gasoline, was used extensively in attempts to burn the Vietcong from their strongholds. Below, a cannister of napalm explodes in a Vietcong-controlled village in the Mekong Delta.

The attack carrier USS Coral Sea waits "on station" in the Gulf of Tonkin. Many of the combat missions flown during the Vietnam War, especially those directed against targets in North Vietnam, were launched from aircraft carriers off the coast.

Right, an Air Force plane sprays the jungle east of Saigon with the defoliant Agent Orange. Agent Orange was used extensively to destroy vegetation that might provide cover for enemy forces. The use of such compounds as white phosporous, napalm, and Agent Orange, which were highly effective but often devastating to Vietcong and civilians alike, provoked worldwide protest.

TET—THE NEW YEAR'S BATTLES

Flares and exploding Vietcong rockets light up the American Air Base at Da Nang in the early morning hours of January 30, 1968—the Vietnamese New Year—as the Communists launch the massive Tet Offensive. More than 100 towns, villages, and military bases were attacked during Tet.

In the first hours of Tet, Vietcong commandos infiltrated the heavily fortified U.S. embassy compound in Saigon. All the attackers were killed or captured in a pitched battle that included not only soldiers but embassy staff. Left, U.S. officials inspect damage to the embassy wall.

Saigon residents, made homeless by the battle, search for possessions in the wreckage of a building. Entire sections of Saigon were destroyed during Tet. Before the offensive, the city had been largely untouched by fighting.

As everyday life continues, a black-pajama-clad Vietcong lies dead in a Saigon Street. The street-to-street, house-to-house fighting in Saigon and Hue seemed to belong more to World War II than to Vietnam.

THE END

American troops, fighting an unpopular war against an enemy that seemed invisible, sometimes vented their rage and frustration on Vietnamese civilians. But the Vietcong, too, could be ruthless in their effort to gain control of the civilian population. This photograph shows a pro-Saigon village being burned by Vietcong. The guerrillas can be seen on the banks of the canal that irrigated the village's rice fields.

DEPARTMENT OF DE

The ultimate tragedy of Vietnam, as of almost any war, was the suffering inflicted on civilians. Many were killed or wounded in the long conflict, and hundreds of thousands were uprooted from their homes. Below, refugees and defeated government troops flee south after the fall of the city of Quang Tri to the North Vietnamese in 1972. The South Vietnamese military proved incapable of holding back the North Vietnamese advance after the American withdrawal.

Bottom, their year-long tour of Vietnam duty at an end, U.S. soldiers leave for ''the World''—the ''in-country'' GIs term for America. For some 58,000 Americans, there would be no homecoming. For many who survived, adjusting to civilian life proved a long and painful process. And for some—crippled physically or emotionally by Vietnam—the war will never truly end.

CHAPTER 50

THE NIXON YEARS

Acknowledging his election as 37th President of the United States in front of the TV cameras early in the morning of November 8, 1969, Richard M. Nixon reminded his audience of a sign he had seen held up by a small girl at a campaign rally in Ohio. "Bring us together," it had read. "That will be the objective of this administration," said the President-elect, "to bring the American people together."

The role of healer was a new one for Nixon, known even to his most ardent admirers until then as a combative partisan. He had had one of the most extraordinarily resilient careers in the history of American politics. He had been elected Congressman and then Senator from California by implying that his Democratic opponents were tainted with Communism. As Vice-President for eight years under Dwight Eisenhower, he had taken on Soviet Premier Nikita Khrushchev in a free-wheeling debate staged in a model kitchen at an American exhibition in Moscow. After he was defeated for the Presidency by John F. Kennedy in 1960 and for governorship in California by the incumbent Democrat, Pat Brown, in 1962, many observers believed his career was over.

PHOTO TRENDS; HY SIMON

Richard M. Nixon and Spiro T. Agnew triumphed for the Republicans in 1968.

President Nixon visited the People's Republic of China early in 1972 for a week of meetings with Chairman Mao Tse-Tung and Premier Chou-enlai. Here, Mrs. Nixon enjoys the Great Wall.

NATIONAL ARCHIVES

But his tenacity and a set of unforeseeable circumstances, including the assassinations of John F. Kennedy and his brother Robert; the crushing defeat of the implacably conservative Republican candidate, Barry Goldwater, in 1964; Lyndon Johnson's stunning decision not to run for reelection in 1968; and the deep divisions fostered by the Vietnam War, combined to lead Nixon to a narrow victory over Vice-President Hubert Humphrey.

"Let us lower our voices," he said in his inaugural address. "For its part, the government will listen." At first he seemed to be succeeding in restoring national calm and moderation. Unlike his predecessor, Lyndon Johnson, who had been forced to decide domestic and foreign issues of great moment during his first hundred days in office, Nixon took time in assembling his Cabinet and

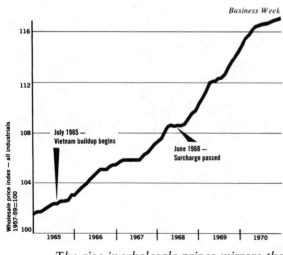

The rise in wholesale prices mirrors the inflation that accompanied escalation of U.S. military involvement in Vietnam.

seemed determined to steer a middle course, especially with regard to the two major issues that confronted him, the war in Southeast Asia and the declining domestic economy.

Nixon's war policy

Like Johnson, Nixon hoped to negotiate his way out of Vietnam rather than either formally declare war or simply withdraw. To demonstrate his good faith and give impetus to the Paris peace talks while defusing antiwar sentiment at home, he began reducing United States forces in the war zone, and secretly sent his national security adviser, Henry Kissinger—soon to become Secretary of State—to Paris to begin talking face-to-face with the chief North Vietnamese negotiator, Le Duc Tho.

But the war showed few signs of abating and the steadily growing number of Americans who opposed it grew increasingly impatient. In April, 1970, the President ordered American troops across Vietnam's western border and into the jungles of neutral Cambodia, where they would find and destroy, he assured the country, "the headquarters for the entire Communist military operation in South Vietnam." This brief extension of the war to another country would, he promised, save American lives and shorten the war itself.

In the long, sad struggle that had gripped Southeast Asia since World War II, the two-month Cambodian invasion did not prove decisive. The promised Communist headquarters could not be found, but large quantities of enemy supplies were discovered, confirming the fact that the North Vietnamese were using bases in a neutral nation to launch attacks into South Vietnam.

But for the antiwar movement, the deliberate widening of an already bloody conflict was unconscionable. Demonstrations erupted anew on college campuses all over the country. Students walked out of classes to attend mass teach-ins devoted to studying the war and finding ways to end it.

Killings at Kent State

When three days of demonstrations at Kent State University in Ohio ended in the burning of the ROTC building there, Governor James Rhodes ordered out the Ohio National Guard in full battle array. A group of some 600 students assembled on campus around noon on May 4. Some jeered at the nervous guardsmen; when others hurled rocks, the guardsmen responded with tear gas. One contingent of guardsmen, cut off from the rest, turned and fired into the students. Four people fell dead: two demonstrators, one ROTC cadet, and one young woman merely walking to class. Nine more students were wounded.

A little over a week later, it happened again, at Jackson State College, a small, mostly black school in Jackson, Mississippi, where two students were shotgunned to death by police.

To many, it seemed as if the Vietnam War had come home to America. One third of the nation's college students began boycotting classes; many schools closed down for the remainder of the academic year. On May 9, 1970, more than one 100,000 demonstrators marched on Washington, demanding an end to the war and carrying signs declaring "This Government Is Deaf."

Meanwhile, small, angry bands of extreme, violent radicals had broken away from the peace movement, among them one called the Weathermen, who stormed through the streets of Chicago smashing store windows and picking fights with police, and whose arsenal of revolutionary techniques included planting bombs. According to one estimate, there were some 5,000 bombings across the country between January, 1960, and April, 1970—only one of which injured an innocent person.

By this time, the Nixon administration had abandoned its goal of quietly soothing the nation. Just five months after taking office, the President had gone on the offensive against those who opposed the war, calling them "new isolationists."

Vice President Spiro T. Agnew, the former Governor of Maryland, was soon thereafter appointed the administration's point man and was assigned the task of promoting what he called "positive polarization," praising "the silent majority," and taunting those whom Nixon and his counselors had come to see as the enemy at home—demonstrators for peace and civil rights, college students, the press, and television.

Nixon had always enjoyed a prickly, adversarial relationship with the press— "You won't have Dick Nixon to kick around anymore," he had told reporters

The slaying of four antiwar Kent State students by Ohio National Guardsmen on May 4, 1970, touched off campus protests throughout the nation.

when he and they both believed his career was at an end in 1962. But in the summer of 1971 his old irritation turned to fury. *The New York Times* published *The Pentagon Papers*—a mammoth, secret Johnson-administration study of how American intervention in Vietnam had begun. Its hundreds of classified documents revealed that the American people had been deliberately misled by Nixon's predecessor in the White House. Nixon himself was untouched by the Johnson-era scandals, but public mistrust of government and opposition to the war inevitably intensified.

The domestic front

Meanwhile, there were other costs to the Vietnam War besides the deepening divisions in American society. The inflation rate, as measured by the Consumer Price Index, had remained below 2% throughout the 1950s and into the early 1960s. Then it had begun to rise, reaching an annual rate of 4.9% in 1970. With inflation slowing the economy, unemployment had increased to an annual rate of almost 5.0% in 1970, and more than 4,000,000 Americans were out of work, the greatest number since the Depression of the 1930s. There would be worse economic news in years to come, but for the first time since the Great Depression, most Americans were beginning to feel a real decline in their standard of living.

In order to pump more money into the slumping economy, the President abandoned the idea of a balanced budget and returned the government to deficit financing. In 1969, the federal government had actually taken in a little over $3 billion more than it spent, creating a small surplus. A small deficit followed in 1970, then in 1971, the deficit leapt to more than $23 billion. In 1972, Nixon took more drastic measures to bring the economy under control. In August, he announced a sweeping program that included a broad 90-day freeze on wages, prices, and rents. Simultaneously, he ended the dollar's convertibility into gold. From now on, the value of the dollar would be free to rise or fall according to trends in the world money markets. He further ordered a 10% surcharge on imports of manufactured goods, and moved to reduce federal expenditures.

These economic measures, the most stringent since the Korean War, were enacted despite Democratic control of both the Senate and the House.

In the midst of the noisy struggle over Vietnam, Nixon's domestic successes were easily overlooked. In his inaugural address, he had proposed a program to begin solving the nation's growing environmental problems; in July, 1970, he established the Environmental Protection Agency. Also during Nixon's first term, an independent U.S. Postal Service was established to replace the increasingly inefficient Cabinet-level Post Office Department, and the Twenty-Sixth Amendment to the Constitution was passed—

A littered highway symbolizes a growing concern to many people—pollution and other menaces to the earth's ecology.

1477

lowering the voting age to 18. The amendment went into effect when Ohio became the 38th state to ratify it, on June 30, 1971.

Nixon goes to China

The President continued his policy of winding down the war in Vietnam into the 1970s. The level of U.S. forces was reduced from its peak of 541,500 in March, 1969, to 156,800 by the end of 1971. While this de-escalation did not generally satisfy domestic critics, it did open the way for important new initiatives with the People's Republic of China and the Soviet Union.

Nixon had been closely identified with the Chinese Nationalist government in Taiwan throughout his career, so when in mid-July, 1971, he announced that he planned to go to Peking, the world was caught off guard. He was setting in motion a dramatic turnaround in official American policy toward China that had kept the two nations apart for more than 20 years. The visit was actually one of a series of moves carefully orchestrated by the Nixon administration and high Chinese officials. A few days after the announcement, Secretary of State William P. Rogers stated that the United States would support China's long-standing bid for membership in the United Nations. In October, the General Assembly voted to seat the People's Republic—and to expel America's longtime ally, Nationalist China. Despite its opposition to the expulsion of the Taiwan government, the United States accepted the General Assembly's actions. Since

China had also been one of the five original "permanent" members of the U.N. Security Council, the People's Republic now took over that seat from Nationalist China. The five permanent members thus became: Britain, Communist China, France, the Soviet Union, and the United States.

Nixon visited China in February, 1972, and while there he met the aging, legendary Chinese leader, Mao Tse-tung and conferred extensively with Premier Chou En-lai. At a sumptuous, televised banquet in the Great Hall of the People, Nixon summarized his hopes for future relations between the two nations: "Neither of us seeks the territory of the other," he said. "Neither of us seeks domination over the other. Neither of us seeks to stretch out our hands and rule the world."

Three months later, he followed his triumph in Peking with a highly productive summit meeting in Moscow with the Soviet leader Leonid I. Brezhnev. Capping the Strategic Arms Limitation Talks (SALT) that had begun in Helsinki, Finland, in 1969, the two countries signed agreements limiting defensive antiballistic missiles (ABMs) and freezing land- and sea-based nuclear weapons at their existing levels. Other agreements provided for closer cooperation in a number of fields, including the environment, medical and health research, and space flight.

The 1972 elections

As the Presidential election of 1972 approached, it became clear that Nixon

President Nixon congratulates astronauts Neil Armstrong, Edwin Aldrin and Michael Collins following their successful Apollo 11 mission to the moon on July 16, 1969. They are speaking from the post-flight quarantine unit.

had built a solid foundation on which to base his campaign for a second term. Though not restored to full health, the nation's economy was on the upswing throughout 1972, performing better than it had at any time since 1967. As election day approached in November, the Dow Jones average reached the 1,000 level for the first time in history. The United States seemed to be edging closer to a settlement of the long Vietnam War, applying pressure on North Vietnam by stepped-up bombing and the mining of Haiphong harbor and other ports, and then renewing efforts at the Paris negotiations. "We believe peace is at hand," Presidential adviser Kissinger an-

nounced confidently in the midst of the campaign.

Nixon and Agnew were renominated by acclamation at the Republican convention in Miami in August; the Democrats found it much harder to agree on their Presidential slate. First came a scramble for votes in the primary elections, which were becoming more and more important in projecting a candidate's image—the names of 11 Democratic contenders appeared on the ballot in Florida alone.

South Dakota Senator George S. McGovern gradually emerged from the primaries and delegate-selection caucuses with an unbeatable number of convention votes. Senator Thomas Eagleton of Missouri was nominated as the Democrats' Vice-Presidential candidate, but was forced to withdraw his name two weeks later when it was disclosed that he had once been hospitalized for a mental condition and had undergone electroshock therapy. He was replaced on the ticket by R. Sargent Shriver, former head of the Peace Corps and brother-in-law of the late President Kennedy.

McGovern declared that if elected he would end the Vietnam War within 90 days of taking office, and he promised amnesty for all those who had gone to prison for draft evasion or left the country to avoid conscription. He also proposed generous new welfare measures and stringent defense cuts that many middle-of-the-road Democrats found unacceptable. Nixon and Agnew skillfully exploited the excesses of McGovern's more extreme supporters to make the Democratic team seem irresponsible and even dangerous.

On election day, Nixon amassed more than 47,000,000 popular votes, the largest number a Presidential candidate had ever received, and won by an electoral landslide of 520 to 17. McGovern carried only Massachusetts and the District of Columbia.

Watergate

In light of Nixon's political strength before, during, and immediately after the 1972 elections, all that happened next in his extraordinary career seemed all the more implausible.

On the night of June 17, 1972, five men had been arrested while burglarizing the headquarters of the Democratic National Committee in the Watergate Office Building in Washington. Judging from the equipment they had with them, it appeared they had intended to install electronic eavesdropping devices in the Democrats' offices. The burglars were identified as employees of the Committee to Reelect the President (CRP), Nixon's campaign committee. Commenting on the matter a few days later, Nixon stated flatly that "there is no White House involvement." He reiterated this point again in late August, insisting, "No one in the White House staff was involved in this very bizarre matter."

But the trail was already leading to the White House. The Watergate burglary team, indicted by a federal grand jury in September, had been led by an ex-FBI and CIA agent named James McCord, who at the time of his arrest, was employed by CRP as director of security. The federal indictment also named CRP staff member G. Gordon Liddy and former White House aide E. Howard Hunt as participants in the crime. McCord and Liddy were promptly fired by CRP's campaign director, former Attorney General John Mitchell. Mitchell himself resigned from CRP a few days after the federal burglary trial began.

Meanwhile, a series of investigative reports by two *Washington Post* reporters, Bob Woodward and Carl Bernstein, named other White House aides involved in illegal campaign activities. The Senate created a Select Committee on Presidential Campaign Activities, headed by Senator Sam J. Ervin (Democrat, North Carolina), to determine if the administration was trying to cover up its role in the burgeoning scandal. Washington came alive with rumors, leaks, sensational newspaper and television reports, and a steady stream of damaging testimony from both the federal burglary trial and Senator Ervin's Select Committee.

In April, President Nixon announced the resignations of several of the highest ranking officials in his administration, including his two closest White House advisers, John Ehrlichman and H.R. Haldeman, Presidential counsel John Dean, acting director of the FBI, L. Patrick Gray, and Attorney General Richard G. Kleindienst. The President nominated Defense Secretary Elliott L. Richardson to replace Kleindienst, and Richardson agreed to Senate demands that he appoint a special Watergate prosecutor to investigate and prepare grand jury indictments covering all the Watergate matters. Archibald Cox, a Harvard law professor and former Solicitor General, was chosen for this job, and he soon began opening up another line of inquiry.

To the further dismay of the nation while Watergate was in the headlines, Vice-President Spiro Agnew was forced to resign his office in October, 1973,

October 10, 1973

Dear Mr. President:

As you are aware, the accusations against me cannot be resolved without a long, divisive and debilitating struggle in the Congress and in the Courts. I have concluded that, painful as it is to me and to my family, it is in the best interests of the Nation that I relinquish the Vice Presidency.

Accordingly, I have today resigned the Office of Vice President of the United States. A copy of the instrument of resignation is enclosed.

It has been a privilege to serve with you. May I express to the American people, through you, my deep gratitude for their confidence in twice electing me to be Vice President.

Sincerely,

/s/ Spiro T. Agnew

The President
The White House
Washington, D.C.

With this letter, dated October 10, 1973, Vice-President Spiro T. Agnew resigned his office.

rather than face charges of bribery, extortion, and income-tax evasion, all unrelated to Watergate. House Minority Leader Gerald R. Ford, an eleven-term Congressman from Grand Rapids, Michigan, was nominated by Nixon to take Agnew's place. His appointment was confirmed by Congress.

The Vietnam peace agreement

In the meantime, Kissinger's 1972 declaration that peace in Vietnam was "at hand" had proved to be premature. Progress at the Paris peace talks had been frustrated by North Vietnam's negotiating tactics after the Presidential elections. "It was clear that the North Vietnamese were sliding away from an agreement," a Kissinger assistant, Winston Lord, later wrote. "Every time we would get close they would slide in new conditions ... they were playing on public opinion, undercutting us at home and stonewalling us in Paris, and there was no choice but to break off negotiations." The talks were discontinued on December 13, 1972.

Five days later, the United States began a massive saturation bombing of North Vietnam on a scale unseen since World War II. For eleven days and nights—pausing only for Christmas—B-52s bombed rail yards, docks, power plants, munitions depots, and petroleum

THE WAR IS OVER!

A CELEBRATION
SHEEP MEADOW
CENTRAL PARK
12:30 P.M. MAY 11, 1975

This poster invited the public to a celebration of the end of the Vietnam War in New York City's Central Park, in May, 1975.

storage areas around Hanoi and Haiphong. In the first night alone, three waves of B-52s—totaling 121 aircraft—struck the two cities. Once again Kissinger and Le Duc Tho resumed their private talks. On the surface, at least, North Vietnam now seemed more willing to negotiate a settlement. On January 22, 1973, an agreement was reached by all parties providing for a cease-fire, the final withdrawal of all U.S. military personnel, the release of all prisoners held by both sides, and the reunification of north and south by peaceful means. The agreement also permitted North Vietnamese soldiers operating in South Vietnam to remain in place. And there they remained, biding their time, waiting for the day, soon to come, when they could topple the South Vietnamese government without further interference from the United States.

The smoking gun

By the summer of 1973, more than a year had passed since the Watergate burglary, and the Senate Select Committee was still taking testimony in its attempt to establish whether or not the President had been responsible for any illegal activities. Special prosecutor Archibald Cox and his team of investigators continued to assemble evidence to present to a grand jury. The search was on for a "smoking gun," as the press called it, a piece of solid evidence that would conclusively link the President to the crimes of his subordinates. The search seemed to be going nowhere until July 16, 1973, a day of otherwise routine testimony before the Senate Select Committee, when a former White House aide, Alexander P. Butterfield, let slip that the President had had conversations in the Oval Office secretly tape recorded. Would these tapes provide the smoking gun?

Special prosecutor Cox moved quickly to subpoena the tapes. Citing "executive privilege," Nixon refused to release them but was rebuffed in a series of federal court decisions. In a last attempt to prevent the release of the tapes, Nixon ordered Attorney General Richardson to fire Cox. In what came to be known as the "Saturday Night Massacre," Richardson resigned rather than comply with the President's order. Deputy Attorney General William D. Ruckelshaus followed suit. The third-ranking official in the Justice Department, Robert H. Bork, then became acting Attorney General and carried out the President's wishes.

Nixon never fully recovered the confidence of the public after that. Eventually, he did turn over a selection of tapes, but two of them were missing and an 18-and-a-half-minute gap in another seemed to blank out a conversation with an aide about Watergate. Nixon appointed a new Attorney General and designated a new Watergate prosecutor, Leon Jaworski, a Texas attorney, who was promised complete independence in his investigations. But by now, the damage was becoming irreversible. When edited transcripts of the tapes were released to the public in April, 1974, they painted a damning picture of plotting and deception at the highest levels.

The Select Committee on Campaign Activities (also known as the Senate Watergate Committee) was formed to investigate the Watergate break-in and coverup. The Committee, led by Senator Sam Ervin (D-N.C.) and staff, seen here, became familiar faces as televised proceedings were watched avidly by millions of Americans around the country.

Impeachment begins

On February 6, 1974, the U.S. House of Representatives authorized an impeachment inquiry by its Judiciary Committee against President Nixon. Over a hundred years had passed since the House had deliberated the evidence against Lincoln's successor, Andrew Johnson, the only other President to face impeachment in the nation's history.

Nixon continued to resist Congressional demands for additional tapes; his lawyers argued in one courtroom after another that the recordings were his to withhold, until it became obvious even to his most loyal supporters that the House Judiciary Committee had sufficient evidence of obstruction of justice to deliver a Bill of Impeachment and recommend that he stand trial before the Senate. Republican Congressional lead-

ers, fearing Nixon would be unlikely to muster enough votes for an acquittal in the Senate, now advised the President to resign. Faced with a unanimous Supreme Court decision calling upon him to turn over further recordings, Nixon elected on August 5 to publish three transcripts of post-Watergate talks with H.R. Haldeman. In one of them, the President ordered that the FBI be kept from investigating Watergate any further. That was the smoking gun, but Nixon's Presidency was already doomed. On August 9, 1974, he resigned from the Presidency, the only chief executive ever to do so. At last, after two years of bluster, leaks, stonewalling, accusations, convictions, and deep and searching public debate about the Presidency and the nature of Constitutional government, a long, painful ordeal was over.

THE WORLD
OF OUTER SPACE

Just as humankind was once impelled to explore the oceans in search of new lands, so we have reached out into the world beyond our own planet. From the early days of unmanned space probes and satellites to the space-shuttle missions of the early 1980s (above), thousands of technicians around the globe have contributed to the struggle to conquer space. Manned space flights and the six successful moon landings have received the most attention, but many other achievements have occurred that would have seemed impossible when the National Aeronautics and Space Administration was created, in 1958—weather observations and intercontinental communications by orbiting satellites, to mention but two. Still, we are not content; despite recent setbacks, research continues, with the next great step, a manned voyage to one of the planets, beginning to emerge on the distant horizon.

THE RUSSIANS ACHIEVED
MANY SPACE "FIRSTS"

Most of the initial successes in space exploration belonged to the Russians, who rightfully took great pride in their accomplishments. Above the Soviet magazine *Krokodil* salutes the world's first space hero, Yuri Gagarin, for his pioneering orbit of the earth on April 12, 1961. In August of that same year Gherman S. Titov made 16 orbits; in 1962, two other Russians made 45 and 60 orbits in a double flight. The cosmonauts were given highest honors and sent on tours of both the Soviet Union and foreign countries to call attention to Russia's achievements and lead in the early days of the space age.

The Russians inaugurated the space age when Sputnik I was launched on October 4, 1957. The first man-made object to be put into orbit, it circled the earth at distances up to 560 miles for three months. In the picture above. taken in East Germany a model of it is on the left; at right is the much more elaborate Sputnik III, which was launched in 1958.

Cosmonaut Gagarin is shown just before take-off. His flight took him in an orbit 108 to 187 miles out, and he reached a top speed of some 17,000 miles an hour—the fastest man had traveled up to that time.

Valentina V. Tereshkova, 26—a former textile worker whose parachuting hobby led her into the Russian space program—was the first woman to orbit the earth, 48 times in just 70 hours and 50 minutes.

MIGHTIEST BOOSTER

Almost from the start of the space race with Russia, the United States set its sights on landing men on the moon. To do so required the development of a rocket capable of carrying a manned craft across 240,000 miles of space and back again. After nearly a decade of work, the three-stage, multiengine Saturn V (being test-fired at right) was perfected. Although the Titan II (seen at left launching Gemini X into earth orbit in 1966) can generate 430,000 pounds of thrust to lift 8,000 pounds into earth orbit, the first stage of the Saturn (below) produces 7,500,000 pounds of thrust.

AMERICA SENDS ITS ASTRONAUTS ALOFT

ALL: NASA

Months of training and testing preceded the first phase of America's manned space program—Project Mercury. Ground simulators, such as the one at left, prepared astronauts for manually controlling their spacecrafts. Pictured here are three U.S. space pioneers: above, Colonel John H. Glenn, Jr., the first American to orbit the earth; below left, Commander Walter M. Schirra, Jr.; below right, Major L. Gordon Cooper, Jr.

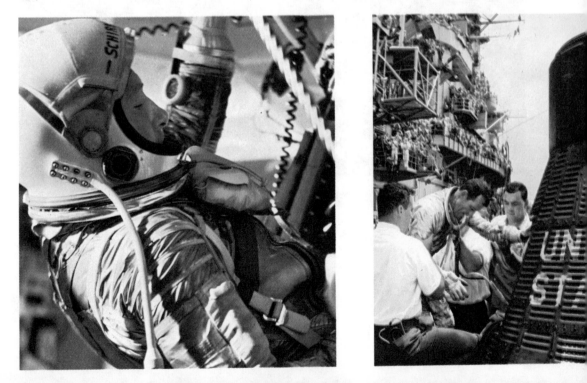

PREPARING FOR THE MOON

If man was to be able to work in space, and not merely revolve in it—a prerequisite for a lunar landing—he had to prove that he could maneuver both himself and his craft while aloft. These were among the objectives of Project Gemini, the second step in America's moon program. From March 23, 1965, until November 11, 1966, ten Gemini flights, each with two astronauts aboard, were launched from the NASA "spaceport" at Cape Kennedy, Florida. Many new records were set: the first manned orbital maneuvers, by Virgil I. Grissom and John W. Young in Gemini III; the first extended manned flight (120 revolutions in eight days), by the Gemini V crew; and the docking of a spacecraft with an orbiting target, by Neil A. Armstrong and David R. Scott aboard Gemini VIII.

ALL: NASA

Thousands of scientists, engineers, and technicians make up the American space team that guides manned flights from 15 NASA installations. Above is a firing room in the Launch Control Center at Cape Kennedy during a before-flight test for Apollo IX.

From 160 miles above the earth Gemini VII (left) is seen through the hatch window of Gemini VI as they rendezvous in December, 1965. Below, Edward H. White II has his picture taken by Gemini IV command pilot James A. McDivitt during his spectacular 21-minute "walk in space" on June 3, 1966. White, though, was not the first man ever to move about in space from an orbiting craft; Russian cosmonaut Aleksei A. Leonov had performed the same feat only three months earlier.

PROJECT APOLLO

In May, 1961, President John F. Kennedy officially committed America to landing a man on the moon and returning him safely to earth "before this decade is out." After a score of successful manned missions, Project Apollo—the final phase of the lunar program—achieved fulfillment. On July 16, 1969, the crew of Apollo XI began their epic-making journey, a trip soon to become common-place. Aboard were (below, left to right) Neil A. Armstrong, commander; Michael Collins, pilot of the command module *Columbia*; and Edwin E. Aldrin, Jr., pilot of the lunar module *Eagle*.

ALL.: NASA

Because the lunar module, which would actually land on the moon, only had to function in airless space and did not have to contend with the earth's atmosphere, engineers were free to design the first nonstreamlined flying vehicle. The result was an ungainly but efficient contraption once described as "a stack of hatboxes piled precariously on top of four spindly legs." The $2,000,000,000 LM, a combination rocket and spacecraft, had been tested in two previous manned missions but had never actually landed anywhere until the Apollo XI flight. Below, Collins, alone in the command ship *Columbia*, photographed the LM on the way to its first touchdown with Armstrong and Aldrin aboard.

MEN ON THE MOON

At 4:17 P.M. (E.D.T.), Neil Armstrong radioed to earth. "Houston. Tranquility Base here—the *Eagle* has landed." Man was on the moon! But history was just beginning to be made. At 10:56 P.M., Armstrong emerged from the LM and became the first man to stand on a celestial body other than the earth. "That's one small step for a man, one giant leap for mankind," he said as he touched the moon's surface. Eighteen minutes later, he photographed Edwin Aldrin (left) backing down the LM's steps. Above, Armstrong, taking another picture, is reflected in Aldrin's visor.

Apollo XI casts its shadow over the southwest section of the moon's Sea of Tranquility. When this photograph was taken, both *Eagle* and *Columbia* were still docked and in a lunar orbit

1498

EXPLORING THE UNKNOWN

One of Neil Armstrong's first tasks on the moon was the planting of a specially constructed U.S. flag. intended, according to the wording of an act of Congress, as a "symbolic gesture of national pride" not a "claim of sovereignty." (The astronauts carried many other flags with them, including those of the 50 states and the United Nations.) Also symbolic of the spirit of the mission was the plaque on the opposite page. Attached to a rung of the ladder of the descent stage, it was left behind with the LM to mark the *Eagle*'s landing spot. The astronauts explored the moon for 2 hours and 13 minutes, collecting about 50 pounds of lunar rocks and soil and conducting a number of scientific experiments. Below, Edwin Aldrin is depicted setting in place instruments to detect ground tremors.

ALL: NASA

THE VOYAGE CONTINUES

Six more manned Apollo flights left Cape Kennedy for the Moon between July 1969 and December 1972. Five of them landed successfully, and each time the astronauts spent more time on the Moon and conducted more extensive experiments, including exploration of the Moon's surface aboard the Lunar Roving Vehicle (LRV). One flight, Apollo 13 of April 1970, was forced to abort following a mechanical failure. After a tense period of uncertainty—the world held its breath for nearly 6 days— the capsule and its three crewmen returned to earth safely.

With the completion of the Apollo program NASA turned its attention to the creation of a semi-permanent orbiting station, in which astronauts could be live and work comfortably for extended periods. The first such vehicle, the 77-ton, 118-foot-long Skylab I, was launched into orbit nearly 270 miles above the Earth on May 14, 1973. Eleven days later an Apollo spacecraft carrying the three-man crew for the station connected with Skylab. A second crew arrived in July. Skylab gathered much valuable information about the Earth and space from its unparalleled vantage point. A third crew, launched in November, spent eighty-four days aboard the space station.

In a dramatic expression of international commitment to peaceful and cooperative space exploration, an American Apollo and a Soviet Soyuz spacecraft linked up in orbit on July 17, 1975, and their crews conducted joint experiments. That same summer, two unmanned Viking probes left the earth, and a year later they touched down on the surface of the planet Mars and sent back photos and data. Similar probes would make "flybys" of Saturn, Jupiter, and Uranus in the decade ahead.

The space-shuttle program occupied NASA throughout late 1970s and early 1980s. A quantum leap in space exploration, the shuttle was the first practical reusable space vehicle. Blasted into space by rockets, the shuttle could return to earth as a glider. In addition to providing a platform for experiments, the shuttle's cargo bay could carry satellites for launching and retrieve damaged satellites for repair. The first shuttle, the Columbia, made its initial flight in 1981. In 1983 the second shuttle, the Discovery, made the first in-orbit satellite repairs. A number of successful flights had been made by January 28, 1986, when, in America's worst space tragedy, the Challenger exploded shortly after lift-off, killing its seven-member crew. Despite this serious setback, NASA continues its efforts toward the exploration of space.

Postage stamps commemorate the joint American and Soviet Apollo-Soyuz test project that took place in the summer of 1975. The rendezvous between American astronauts and Soviet cosmonauts was the first such international space mission in history.

Looking remarkably similar to some of the earth's own desert regions, this is the surface of the planet Mars as seen in one of the photos transmitted back to earth by the unmanned Viking II probe in the Summer of 1976.

Seven months after the Challenger tragedy, a new version of the space shuttle's solid-fuel rocket booster is test-fired in Utah. After extensive investigations, NASA discovered that a broken seal, combined with unseasonably cold temperatures and a faulty launch procedure, had caused the disaster.

1501

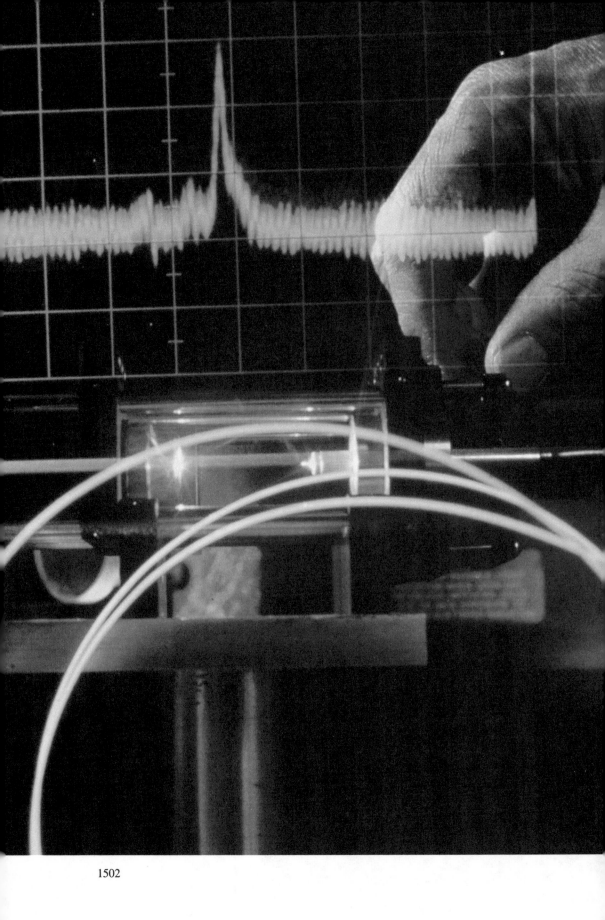

CHAPTER 51

THE ONRUSH OF TECHNOLOGY

The first view of the planet earth was breathtaking. Coasting above the broad, barren plains of the moon, the crew of *Apollo 10* focused a color television camera on the moon's horizon. As millions watched, the earth began to rise, a beautiful blue planet against the black sky of outer space.

This moment of high drama took place in May, 1969, in the program that a few weeks later would land a man on the moon. And, though many did not realize it at the time, the earth's first color portrait from space was also a triumph of high technology—the culmination of a torrent of breakthroughs, great and small, in computers, communications, space flight, and many other disciplines. In the language of space flight, all systems were go for even more spectacular achievements, not just in space alone, but in areas that would greatly affect everyday life in the United States in thousands of unforeseen ways.

In its short history, the United States has experienced two major technological revolutions. The first came in agriculture, where inventions such as the reaper and the cotton gin transformed the production of food and fiber and laid the foundation for America's preeminence as an agricultural nation. A second, even more sweeping wave of technological innovation began in the second half of the nineteenth century and extended into the early years of the twentieth. During this period the very face of the nation was transformed by railroads, mass production of steel and other goods, electrification, and, ultimately, the automobile and the airplane. The social and economic consequences of this second revolution were even greater than those of the first.

Laser technology has come to play an increasing role in communications. Pictured here is optical diagnostic equipment that uses lasers to monitor the temperatures of orbiting space shuttles.

The computer's impact

A third technological revolution started in the late 1940s. This revolution was born in the research laboratories of

Pictured here is a Polaroid founder Edward Land, inventor of a one-step photographic process which allowed amateur photographers to see their photos in a matter of minutes, revolutionizing photography as a hobby.

World War II and its most visible fruit, the computer, began to reach maturity in the 1950s and 60s, as extremely sophisticated systems became necessary to guide military missiles and civilian spacecraft. Computers became smaller and cheaper in the 1970s and spread almost explosively into other fields. The boom shows no signs so far of slowing down, and yet the third revolution is still so new that even the experts are not exactly sure about what to call it. Is it the dawning of the Information Age, or the Computer Era, or is it something else? A similar uncertainty exists about where the third revolution is heading. But there is no doubt now that this new technological revolution already has had an enormous impact on all walks of life.

The United States continues to lead the world in computer technology, although nations such as Japan are challenging this leadership in the manufacture of chips and in other specific areas. There is probably no segment of technology where being first is more important than in computers. "In the headlong rush of high technology," said a 1987 special report in *Fortune* magazine, "the driving force has been the computer and everything connected with it—semiconductor chips, robots, telecommunications. By the year 2000 the electronics industry, already a $300-billion-a-year business, should become the biggest in the world except for agriculture. The nation that dominates it will stand astride the world economy."

The heart of high technology is the digital computer. The word digital is significant, for in a digital computer all basic operations are carried out using only two numbers, 0 and 1. These two numbers really represent "on" or "off" signals, or plus or minus electrical charges. Zeros and ones are assembled into "bytes," strings that together signify numerals, letters of the alphabet, or special symbols when processed by the computer. The digital form of data processing is highly reliable and very fast because all operations are carried out by simply flipping 1s to 0s back and forth, and this takes place almost at the speed of light. By joining many circuits together, computers can carry out millions—even billions—of calculations per second.

The first digital computers were very slow, difficult to use, and had a bad habit of breaking down in the midst of important problems. ENIAC, completed at the University of Pennsylvania in late 1945, contained 17,468 vacuum tubes and 6,000 manual switches. Large air blowers were needed to prevent the vacuum tubes from overheating and failing. But the concepts behind the ENIAC's design were sound, and government agencies and commercial companies with huge data-processing requirements began to get interested. Soon to follow was UNIVAC, developed for Remington Rand by two of the men who had produced ENIAC: J. Presper Eckert, Jr., and John Mauchly. In March, 1951, the first UNIVAC computer was delivered to the U.S. Census Bureau. Forty-six of the huge machines were installed by American businesses by 1956.

Enter IBM

International Business Machines (IBM) was already a large, successful company when it ventured into the computer field in the 1950s. IBM's specialty was punch-card data-processing systems, and by 1945 IBM was number one in the business-machine industry with revenues of $141,700,000. IBM's growth between 1946 and 1955 averaged an astonishing 22% per year, but though most corporate chief executives would have been satisfied with this kind of record, Thomas J. Watson, Jr., wasn't. Watson, the son of IBM's founder, be-

During the early 1950s, the computer was still a complex and remote technology, requiring major hardware and highly trained technicians (above) for operations now routinely performed on desk-top personal computers.

came chief executive officer in 1956 and sensed correctly that the future of his business lay in computers.

IBM moved slowly at first, concentrating on assignments for the U.S. government, whose growing national defense requirements were creating a need for increasingly sophisticated computers. IBM was the prime contractor for the Air Force on the SAGE air defense system in the early 1950s. IBM then developed a large general-purpose computer, the IBM 701, with government backing. The first IBM 701 was delivered to the Los Alamos Scientific Laboratory in March, 1953. IBM eventualy delivered 18 701s—four to government agencies, eight to aircraft manufacturers also deeply involved in government work, three to universities, and three to large corporations such as General Elec-

tric and General Motors. New lines of IBM computers followed the 701, and the company grew at an annual rate of 16% from 1955 to 1970, with annual revenues reaching $7.5 billion in 1970. By 1983, IBM's annual sales had risen to $40 billion. But it was no longer the fastest growing company in the computer business.

During this period, transistors had replaced vacuum tubes in everything from computers to portable radios. And even more important for making computers smaller and cheaper, the integrated circuit (IC) or "chip" had been developed. Introduced commercially in 1961 by Fairchild Semiconductor and Texas Instruments, the IC is a tiny, wafer-like component in which layers of specially treated silicon are arranged so that several different types of tiny electrical circuits can be contained in the chip without interfering with one another. In late 1971, the Intel Corporation introduced the 4004 "microprocessor" chip that contained the circuitry of a complete computer in a sandwich of silicon less than one-quarter inch square. The 4004 microprocessor could carry about 60,000 operations per second. By 1985, Intel was producing microprocessor chips that could handle 5,000,000 instructions per second.

This device, computer historian Stan Augarten points out, "would become the universal motor of electronics. . . . It could be placed inexpensively and unobtrusively in all sorts of devices—a washing machine, a gas pump, a butcher's scale, a jukebox, a typewriter, a

Desk-top personal computer in operation.

doorbell, a thermostat.'' Very quickly the digital computer was evolving from the rows of large machines that monitored space-flight telemetry and made possible pictures of the earth as seen from the moon, into something that could fit on the top of a desk.

Apple Computer

The rise of Apple Computer is one of the most remarkable success stories in American history. Intrigued by the potential of computers and fascinated by the possibilities of the ICs which were just coming onto the market, two young college dropouts, Steven Jobs and Stephen Wozniak, began experimenting with designs for a small computer in California in 1975. Both had been electronics hobbyists since childhood. Jobs worked as a video-game designer for Atari; Wozniak was a computer programmer for Hewlett-Packard. Their first joint effort was a crude computer circuit board that could be programmed and hooked to a monitor or television set. The device was relatively cheap—$666.66—and appealed immediately to electronics hobbyists in the San Francisco Bay Area. With orders for 100 boards from an electronics store that catered to hobbyists, Jobs and Wozniak set up the Apple Computer Company in a garage behind Steve Jobs's house. While Wozniak perfected the Apple II computer—an expanded and much easier-to-use version of the original Apple I circuit board—Jobs obtained financing for the production of Apple II. It was introduced in 1977 to a public hun-

Steven Jobs and Stephen Wozniak, the whiz-kids who founded Apple Computer, are seen here with the MacIntosh, a top-of-the-line personal computer known for its sophisticated graphic capabilities.

gering for personal computers. Sales soared from $775,000 in 1977 to $335,000,000 in 1981, making Apple the fastest growing corporation in American history. Steve Jobs turned 26 in 1981, Wozniak was 31 that year.

As the hobbyists' plaything moved out into the general public in large numbers, the business of designing, manufacturing, and marketing computers and their software expanded greatly and created ripples that were felt far beyond the basic industry itself. Graphics developed for computer video games, for example, led to astonishing new special effects in movies such as *Star Wars,* the second biggest money-making film of all time (*E.T. The Extra-Terrestrial* ranks first).

Professional writers turned to computer word processing as a substitute for typewriters and soon began producing electronic copy on floppy disks that could be used much more efficiently by computers to set type for books, such as this volume in the *American Heritage Illustrated History of the United States* and most other books published today. In schools, even kindergarten children began to hone their reading and writing with educational software that combined simple word processing with graphic elements like those found in video games. The computer did not replace the classroom teacher, but it proved highly effective in reinforcing teachers' lessons.

The impact of large, "mainframe" computers has been even greater, especially when linked to other high-technology developments. In air-traffic control, for instance, the link is between computers and radar. Every jet airliner is guided through the crowded skies by human air-traffic controllers, but the range of the human eye is extended hundreds of miles by radar. The incoming radar signals are fed into computers that alert controllers whenever planes are predicted to be coming too close to each other, and the air-traffic controllers can then direct the pilots to change courses or altitudes. In oil refineries, steel mills, and nuclear power plants, sophisticated instruments constantly monitor processes that are too dangerous or compli-

Computer technology is effecting great changes in industrial manufacturing. Here, robots operate an assembly line at a Ford Motor Company plant in Michigan.